ASTROLOGY
COLORING BOOK

ASTROLOGY
COLORING BOOK

SIRIUS

This edition published in 2023 by Sirius Publishing, a division of
Arcturus Publishing Limited,
26/27 Bickels Yard, 151–153 Bermondsey Street,
London SE1 3HA

ISBN: 978-1-3988-3017-2
CH011162NT

Printed in China

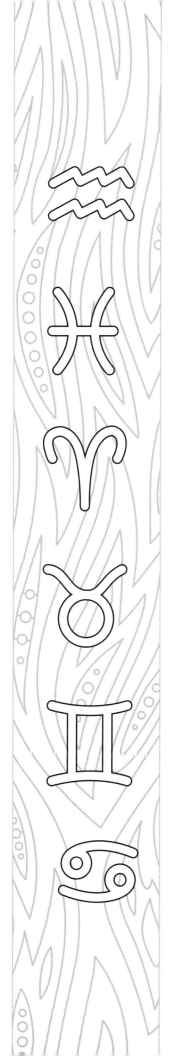

Introduction

In astrology, the time and place you were born will determine your star sign. The placement of the planets will show you what your day, week, or month will be like—for example whether there is anything or anyone you should avoid—and if it will be a happy time or a more difficult occasion.

Collected in the pages of this book are various styles and depictions of the astrological signs. Some are simple, while others are complex and highly detailed. Whether you chart the planets and follow celestial events or simply enjoy reading the general information about your personality and the way you interact with others, this book offers all the star signs in a range of designs for you to color.

So, find the perfect place and time, grab your colored medium of choice, and begin to discover yourself in a new way.

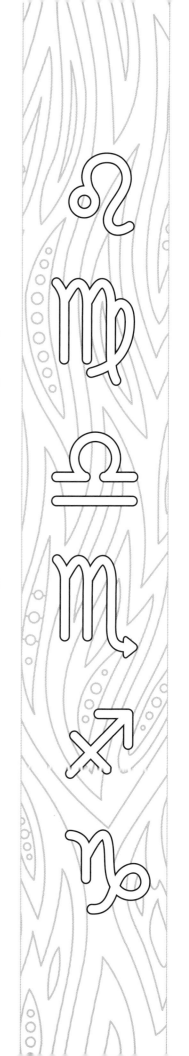

AQUARIUS

ARIES

PISCES

TAURUS

GEMINI

CANCER

LEO

VIRGO

LIBRA

SCORPIO

SAGITTARIUS

CAPRICORN

TAURUS

GEMINI

CANCER

LEO

VIRGO

LIBRA

SCORPIO

SAGITTARIUS

CAPRICORN

AQUARIUS

PISCES

ARIES

TAURUS

GEMINI

CANCER

LEO

VIRGO

SCORPIO

SAGITTARIUS

CAPRICORN

PISCES

AQUARIUS

PISCES

ARIES

TAURUS

GEMINI

CANCER

LEO

VIRGO

LIBRA

SCORPIO

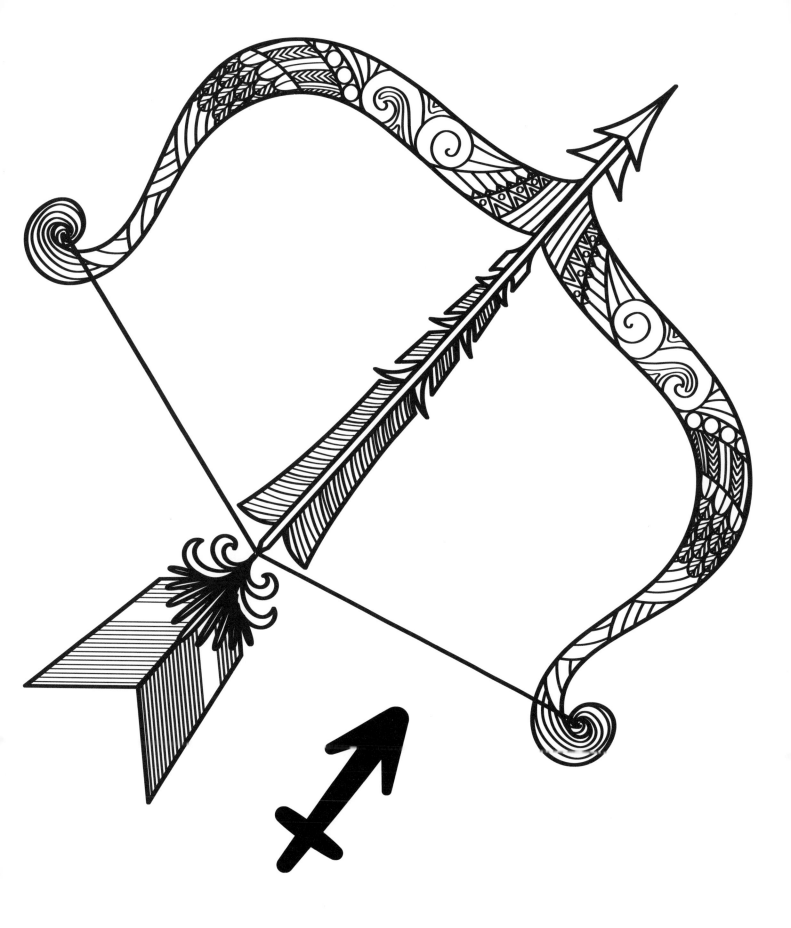

SAGITTARIUS

CAPRICORN

ARIES

TAURUS

GEMINI

CANCER

LEO

VIRGO

LIBRA

SCORPIO

SAGITTARIUS

CAPRICORN

AQUARIUS

PISCES

ARIES

TAURUS

GEMINI

CANCER

LEO

VIRGO

LIBRA

SCORPIO

SAGITTARIUS

CAPRICORN

AQUARIUS

PISCES